# How the Bible Influences You

Woodrow Kroll

**BACK TO THE BIBLE**
LINCOLN, NE 68501

17,000 printed to date—1995
(1150-222—4M—55)
ISBN 0-8474-0892-2

Unless otherwise noted, all Scripture quotations are from
*The New King James Version.*

Printed in the United States of America.

# Introduction

A rough and uncultured man walked by a store window. Through the glass he saw a beautiful vase, which he fell in love with immediately. He bought the vase, took it home and put it on the mantelpiece in his living room.

But there the beautiful vase became a judgment on its surroundings. The curtains looked dingy beside it. The old chair with the stuffing spurting out of the seat had to go. The walls needed new wallpaper and paint. Gradually, the man transformed the whole living room to make it worthy of the vase.

That's the power of influence. It's the kind of influence the Bible has on everyone who takes it seriously. If you allow the Bible to be more than a treasured book, more than an ornament of your faith, if you allow the Bible to influence you, it will change every area of your life.

As you read this book, consider how the Bible can change your life and the way you look at the world.

# Chapter 1

# The Bible Influences
# Your Thinking

Our days are filled with thoughts great and small. We ponder the big questions of life—"Where did I come from?"—and the little ones— "What should I wear today?"

The influence of the Bible should be brought to bear on every area of life. Does the Bible influence everything you think about? Here are some examples of the things we think about that should be filtered through the pages of God's Word.

### How did it all begin?

Do you ever think about how this world came into being? If you do, where do you get your ideas? What influences your thinking about how it all began?

Perhaps you've been influenced by a college professor or by something you saw on television. Maybe you've been influenced by a book you read. But what about the Bible? If it has influenced your thinking, you'll view this question very differently.

For one thing, the Bible begins with a simple statement about how it all began. "In the beginning God created the heavens and the earth" (Gen. 1:1). Though that statement has been frequently ridiculed, no one ever has disproved it.

The Bible is very clear. There was a creator to everything, and that creator was not an impersonal force; that creator was God.

C. S. Lewis observed, "Science, when it becomes perfect, will have explained the connection between each link in the chain and the link before it. But the actual existence of the chain will remain wholly unaccountable." [1]

If you allow the Bible to influence your thinking, you'll have a very different explanation for how we got here than most people have, but you'll have the right one.

---

"I find more sure marks of
authenticity in the Bible than in
any profane history whatsoever."
—Sir Isaac Newton

---

## How will it all end?

What about the other end of history? Have you allowed the Bible to influence your thinking about how the human drama will end?

Without the Bible we would be left to those tabloids you see at supermarket checkouts. Not much comfort there—not to mention believability! But when the Bible influences your thinking you have hope—hope in Jesus' return, hope in heaven and hope in eternity with the Savior.

Jesus said, "I go to prepare a place for you. And if I go and prepare a place for you, I will come again and receive you to Myself; that where I am, there you may be also" (John 14:3).

All history is rushing toward a definite climax, and only the Bible has the proper insight on what that climax is. Our preparation for that climax is influenced by Jesus' words, recorded in the Bible, "Behold, I am coming quickly! Blessed is he who keeps the words of the prophecy of this book" (Rev. 22:7).

If you allow the Bible to influence you, it will cause you to think differently about origins and ends. But there's more.

## What do you think about your family?

The importance of the family is rooted in the Bible. God created the family, and He sanctified it. Society sometimes appears to be destroying the family, but we can protect our families if we think biblically.

This is illustrated in the book *Balancing Life's Demands,* by J. Grant Howard. He wrote, "One evening after supper, I settled into my easy chair with a good book and began to immerse myself in its stimulating, stretching, theological insights. Down the hall and into the room came our 3-year-old bombshell, Juli.

"'Daddy,' she said, 'will you read to me?'

"I looked at the book I was reading—*The Providence of God,* by G. C. Berkouwer, translated from the Dutch. I looked at the book she was holding in her pudgy little hand—*Myrtle the Turtle*. That's when love stops being sentiment and theory. . . . That night I sacrificed Berkouwer for Myrtle."

7

Real parental love is biblical love because it takes its cue from God's great love for us. When you filter your view of family life through the influence of the Bible, you will view your family differently. It's only when we get back to the Bible that we put the proper focus on the family.

## What do you think about society?

We all sympathize with the poor girl who spent four years learning how to behave in polite society and the rest of her life trying to locate it.

What do you think about society? Should it influence you, or should you influence it? The truth is that it works both ways. But sometimes society influences us in ways the Bible never intended.

In our materialistic society, many people spend much of their time trying to get their share of the material. That's not evidence of biblical thinking.

When we are influenced by God's Word, not only will we know which of society's influences are pleasing to God and which are not, but we will have a positive influence on our society. People will know we have lived in their world.

Jesus said it this way: "You are the salt of the earth; but if the salt loses its flavor, how shall it be seasoned? . . . You are the light of the world. A city that is set on a hill cannot be hidden. . . . Let your light so shine before men, that they may see your good works and glorify your Father in heaven" (Matt. 5:13–14, 16).

If you are influenced by the Bible, your neighbors will know. You can't hide it. You'll be salt and light. The people you work with will know. Expect some of your thinking to fly in the face of society when your thinking is influenced by the Bible. That certainly was true of Jesus.

But don't worry. Our society needs more people whose thinking is influenced by the Bible. Don't fail to be one of them.

[1] *God in the Dock*, "The Laws of Nature," p. 78.

# Chapter 2

# The Bible Influences Your Living

If the Bible influences how you think, and how you think influences how you live, the Bible influences your living as well as your thinking.

This doesn't happen 100 percent of the time, of course, because no one lets the Bible influence his thinking 100 percent of the time. But there is a good reason to allow the Bible to influence your living.

Christians are engaged in a fierce battle against the forces of Satan. You and I are only foot soldiers in this battle, but we do have a war manual to give us strategies and orders. That manual is the Bible.

## Guidelines for spiritual warfare

In preparing us for spiritual warfare, the Bible not only lists our battle equipment, it is part of our equipment. Ephesians 6 describes our armor for spiritual warfare:

> *Therefore put on the full armor of God, so that*
> *when the day of evil comes, you may be able to*

*stand your ground, and after you have done
everything, to stand. Stand firm then, with the
belt of truth buckled around your waist, with the
breastplate of righteousness in place, and with
your feet fitted with the readiness that comes from
the gospel of peace. In addition to all this, take up
the shield of faith, with which you can extinguish
all the flaming arrows of the evil one. Take the
helmet of salvation and the sword of the Spirit,
which is the word of God* (Eph. 6:13-17, NIV).

In his book *A Thinking Man's Guide to Pro Football*,
Paul Zimmerman quotes a physicist who made a
rather startling discovery. When a 240-pound football lineman (capable of running 100 yards in 11 seconds) collides with a 240-pound running back (capable of covering the same distance in 10 seconds), the
resultant kinetic energy is "enough to move 66,000
pounds—or 33 tons—one inch." The scientist further
says that in all likelihood, the collision would deliver
to the player's helmet a blow nearly 1,000 times the
force of gravity.

Obviously, modern football helmets have to withstand tremendous blows, or no player would survive
long. But the soldier in the Lord's army has better
equipment than that. Allow the way you live to be
influenced by the Bible, and you will have state-of-
the-art armor to withstand the schemes of the devil.

## Guidelines for living by faith

When we are influenced by the Bible to live by faith
we look at the future differently. Every tomorrow has
two handles. We can take hold of it by the handle of

anxiety or by the handle of faith. The influence of the Bible helps us grab hold of the future by faith.

But we need concrete examples if we're going to live by faith, and the best examples are in the Bible. God's Word not only defines living by faith, it demonstrates it in the lives of people.

"By faith Noah, being divinely warned of things not yet seen, moved with godly fear, prepared an ark for the saving of his household" (Heb. 11:7).

"By faith Abraham obeyed when he was called to go out to the place which he would afterward receive as an inheritance. And he went out, not knowing where he was going" (v. 8).

There are many more, but perhaps you're thinking, *These are all superheroes. I'm not like them. I can't live like that.*

Kids today watch cartoons on television just like I did as a kid, but the cartoons are different. Today the hot cartoons are Captain Planet and other super-heroes. Children have no trouble "being" their favorite superhero. They believe they can do anything their superheroes can do.

So what's the matter with us as adults? Have we just become realists, or do we have an appalling lack of faith? Remember what Jesus said: We must come to Him in faith as a little child if we are to enter the kingdom of God (Luke 18:17).

When you allow the Bible to influence your living, it will help you live by faith, the way your "super-heroes" of the Scriptures did.

### Guidelines for grace living

The Bible also influences us in living grace-filled lives. We live the grace life when we recognize we are saved by grace and that we're to live as we were saved.

Living the life of grace means living a life of freedom in Christ Jesus. We are awakened by grace and remember that we are no longer bound by the law.

Paul told the Galatian Christians, "Stand fast therefore in the liberty by which Christ has made us free, and do not be entangled again with a yoke of bondage" (Gal. 5:1). By that he meant that our new life in Christ is not the binding kind of life people had under the Mosaic law. Christ has freed us from the curse of the law.

---

"Why will people go astray when they have this blessed Book to guide them?"   —Michael Faraday

---

The principles of the law are good and helpful in governing society.  But we are no longer bound to those principles for the support of spiritual life. Now we are bound to Christ. We draw our spiritual life from Him. "I have been crucified with Christ; it is no longer I who live, but Christ lives in me; and the life which I now live in the flesh I live by faith in the Son of God, who loved me and gave Himself for me" (Gal. 2:20).

Second Peter 3:18 says, "But grow in the grace and knowledge of our Lord and Savior Jesus Christ." And Colossians 3:16 adds, "Let the Word of Christ dwell in you richly in all wisdom, teaching and admonishing one another in psalms and hymns and spiritual songs, singing with grace in your hearts to the Lord."

Did you notice the connection between the Bible and grace? The Bible puts a song in our hearts. The Bible brings grace to our lives. As we are influenced by God's Word, we live a life of grace.

When the Bible does not influence us, we lapse back into a legal system of living rather than God's grace system. So let the Bible influence your daily living and you'll live a life of grace.

# Chapter 3

# The Bible Influences Your Values

Each of us has a value system. We judge every-thing in life by that system. But what if our system is flawed? What does that say about our judgment? If you allow the Bible to influence your values, any judgment you make that is filtered through the truths of the Bible will never be flawed.

Here are some areas of your value system that need to be judged against God's Word.

## Lifetime goals

If a reporter stopped you on the street and asked, "What is your major goal in life?" what would you answer? For most people the answer is to make money or live comfortably. For others it's just to get by.

But when your values are influenced by the Bible, your goals change. Solomon concluded the Book of Ecclesiastes with these words: "Fear God and keep His commandments, for this is the whole duty of man" (Eccl. 12:13). For the Christian, our highest goal is to reflect the glory of God back to Him, to please Him in every aspect of our lives.

On March 27, 1808, a grand performance of *The Creation* took place in Vienna. The composer, Franz Joseph Haydn, was able to attend, although at 76 he had to be wheeled into the theater in a chair.

Haydn's presence aroused intense enthusiasm among the audience. When the chorus and orchestra burst into the passage, "And there was light," amid the tumult of applause from the enraptured audience, the old composer was seen striving to raise himself. He cried out, "No, no! Not for me, but," pointing to heaven, "from there—from heaven above—comes all!" Then he fell back on his chair, faint and exhausted, and had to be carried out of the room.

What a humble acknowledgment that God alone is worthy of our praise. Haydn's lifetime goal was to reflect God's glory back to Him. He did that through music. How are you doing it?

## Moral absolutes

But the Bible influences us in other ways, too; specifically, in what we view as right and wrong. When you filter your value system through what God has revealed in His Word, you arrive at biblical values. Never has a biblical value system been more necessary than now.

In 1990 Joseph Josephson released a study entitled "The Ethics of American Youth: A Report on the Values and Behaviors of the 18-30 Generation." The author says that an unprecedented proportion of today's young people lacks commitment to core moral values such as honesty, respect for others and personal responsibility.

Cheating is rampant in high schools and colleges. Several studies show that about 75 percent of high school students admit to cheating; about 50 percent of college students cheat regularly. But it's not just the kids. According to a story in the *Los Angeles Times*, experts on resume fraud say that anywhere from 12 percent to 30 percent of resumes contain "deliberate inaccuracies." [1]

> "Without the Bible the education
> of a child in the present state
> of society is impossible."
> —Leo Tolstoy

Compare what the world tolerates, even encourages, with what the Lord hates. The Bible says, "These six things the LORD hates, yes, seven are an abomination to Him: a proud look, a lying tongue, hands that shed innocent blood, a heart that devises wicked plans, feet that are swift in running to evil, a false witness who speaks lies, and one who sows discord among brethren" (Prov. 6:16–19).

Thinking biblically means holding a value system that reflects the pure mind of God, not the corrupt minds of men. If you allow the Bible to influence your values, you may find your value system in stark contrast with those around you, but it will be in line with the One above you.

## Christian lifestyle

How we choose to live tells the world volumes about what our values are. We hear a lot today about traditional family values. For some people that simply means harkening back to a simpler time. For others it means certain political values.

But traditional values and family values that are not biblical values are no dearer to the heart of God than any other values. We need to be influenced by the values of the Bible in the way we live.

Proverbs 4:14 and 18 warn us, "Do not enter the path of the wicked. And do not walk in the way of evil. . . . But the path of the just is like the shining sun, that shines ever brighter unto the perfect day." And Psalm 1:1–2 says, "Blessed is the man who walks not in the counsel of the ungodly, nor stands in the path of sinners, nor sits in the seat of the scornful; but his delight is in the law of the LORD, and in His law he meditates day and night."

Notice the relationship between the "law of the Lord," which is a synonym for the Bible, and a lifestyle value system that pleases God. Only the Word of God can set a proper agenda for our lifestyle.

You can avoid the swamps and quagmires of sin, but only if the Word of God is a lamp to your feet and a light to your path (Ps. 119:105). Absorb as much of God's Word as you can and let it influence the way you choose to live. That's how to win God's blessing.

## Eternal values

The more you read the Bible, the more you identify the kinds of values that are eternal rather than temporal. Being influenced by the Bible will help you clarify the eternals in your life.

Years ago I went to a garage sale and bought an old ceramic jug. On it I painted the words of Mark

8:36: "For what will it profit a man if he gains the whole world, and loses his own soul?" I set the jug on my front porch as a silent witness to all who came to my door that in this house lived a family whose values had been influenced by eternity. We likely weren't going to gain the whole world, and we didn't care. Biblical values determined what we bought, where we went, what we did—everything in our lives.

Has the Bible influenced your thinking to the point that you are no longer spending all your money on this life? Has it influenced your thinking to where you are looking for ways to invest in eternity, instead of spending in time?

A little chorus that my good friend Al Smith wrote is so appropriate:

> *With eternity's values in view, Lord,*
> *with eternity's values in view—*
> *May I do each day's work for Jesus*
> *with eternity's values in view.*

[1] *Los Angeles Times*, October 28, 1990.

# Chapter 4

# The Bible Influences
# Your Destiny

The greatest influence the Bible has on men and women is on their destiny. If you read and heed the Bible, not only will your thinking and values change, your future will change as well.

Let's explore three areas in which the Bible influences your thinking about destiny.

### The eternal bliss of heaven

The Bible has a lot to say about heaven. Included in what we call "heaven" is the home of God, the place of eternal rest and the New Jerusalem.

Heaven is where Jesus is, and if we have trusted Him as Savior, it's where we'll be throughout eternity. He told his disciples, "I go to prepare a place for you" (John 14:2), and then He promised to take them—and all Christians—to that place so we could be with Him forever.

In heaven we will have bodies suited for eternity. They won't decay; they won't get any older; they won't rust or wear out. They will be heavenly bodies in every sense of the word (1 Cor. 15:42-49).

In heaven we will share the glory of Christ (Rom. 5:2) and receive our share of Jesus' inheritance. After all, we are heirs of God and joint-heirs with Christ (8:17). And that inheritance, like our bodies, will be incorruptible; it will never fade or diminish. Unlike stock or precious metals, our estate in heaven will never decrease in value.

But the greatest thing about heaven is that we will be with Jesus, who loved us and gave Himself for us. He is what makes heaven heaven.

Hymnwriter Fanny Crosby captured the joy of seeing Jesus in her hymn "My Savior First of All":

> *When my life-work is ended and I cross the*
>     *swelling tide,*
> *when the bright and glorious morning I shall see,*
> *I shall know my Redeemer when I reach the other*
>     *side,*
> *and His smile will be the first to welcome me.*

If you let the Bible influence your thinking about destiny, you'll conclude that heaven is not a figment of the apostles' imagination. Heaven is a real place because Jesus is a real Savior.

### The eternal damnation of hell

But there's a darker side to what the Bible teaches us about our destiny. Not everyone will be allowed into heaven, because hell awaits those who have died without asking Jesus to forgive their sins.

Hell was not prepared for Christians; it was prepared for Satan and his angels because of their initial rebellion against God (Matt. 25:41). Hell is always described not as a place of the dead—that's Hades—but as a place of everlasting fire and destruction. Hades is where the unsaved go when they die to await their resurrection, judgment and final doom. The English word *hell* should be used exclusively of the lake of fire, the place of final doom for the unsaved.

The Bible depicts hell as a place of torment. Jesus described it as a place where "the fire that shall never be quenched—where their worm does not die and the fire is not quenched" (Mark 9:43–44).

The unsaved in hell experience continuous conscious suffering (Rev. 14:10–11). In Matthew 13:42, Jesus referred to the lawless being cast into the furnace of fire, where there will be "wailing and gnashing of teeth."

---

"It is impossible to mentally or socially enslave a Bible-reading people."    —Horace Greeley

---

What do you know about hell? Where did you get your information? If you listen to friends, you may think hell is a place where you'll see your old buddies and have a good time. But the Bible changes your thinking about hell. It is not a big party for those who like to party. Hell is no laughing matter. The Bible says it is a place where a person never dies, is never annihilated and never receives any relief from the tortures of punishment.

In hell there will be no social communication between people, only stark loneliness. In fact, the worst thing about hell will be the isolation.

If you allow the Bible to influence your thinking, you won't believe the foolish things people say about hell. The Bible says that the Lord Jesus will be "revealed from heaven with His mighty angels in flaming fire taking vengeance on those who do not know God, and on those who do not obey the gospel of our Lord Jesus Christ. These shall be punished with everlasting destruction from the presence of the Lord and from the glory of His power" (2 Thess. 1:7–9).

That's an awful picture, but hell is an awful place. And the most awful thing about hell is that God won't be there. If the presence of Jesus is what makes heaven heaven, His absence is what makes hell hell. Separation from God forever, with no hope of having your destiny reversed, is the worst form of hell.

## Eternal salvation from God

If you let the Bible influence your thinking, however, you will know that you don't have to experience hell.

The Bible says that it is possible for you to go to heaven. You can escape hell and enjoy forever the pleasures of heaven. But Scripture is very clear that there is only one way that can be done. Here's how.

1. Everyone has sinned. "For all have sinned and fall short of the glory of God" (Rom. 3:23). That means me, you—everybody. We all have sinned, and we are all unrighteous. "There is none righteous, no, not one" (v. 10).

2. Because we have sinned we must suffer the consequences, which is death. "The soul who sins shall die" (Ezek. 18:4, 20). "For the wages of sin is death, but the gift of God is eternal life in Christ Jesus our Lord" (Rom. 6:23).

That death is not just physical but spiritual and eternal as well. Ultimately, that means hell. "Then Death and Hades were cast into the lake of fire. This is the second death. And anyone not found written in the Book of Life was cast into the lake of fire" (Rev. 20:14–15).

3. It is possible to avoid the punishment of the lake of fire. How? Obey the Gospel, which is this: "For God so loved the world that He gave His only Begotten Son, that whosoever believes on Him shall not perish, but have everlasting life" (John 3:16). God sent Jesus to die on Calvary's cross to pay the penalty for your sin so you could go to heaven.

So what must you do to be saved from hell?

4. You must believe on the Lord Jesus Christ (Acts 16:31). Believe that your sin against God results in eternal death (hell), but also believe that Jesus died to pay the penalty for your sin and give you eternal life (heaven). The Bible says that when you trust what Jesus did at Calvary for you as all that is necessary for your salvation, you will be saved and your destiny will be changed from hell to heaven.

Do you believe what the Bible says? Do you believe that if you asked Jesus Christ to be your Savior, He would save you from hell? If you do, why not ask Him to save you right now, right where you are. Just pray this little prayer:

"Dear Father, I know I'm a sinner, and I know I can't save myself. I trust what Jesus did for me at Calvary to be all I need to save me from the penalty of hell. Right now I'm asking Jesus Christ to save me from my sin. Thank you for saving me, Father, in Jesus' name, Amen."

If you have just trusted Jesus to be your Savior, you have allowed the Bible to be the ultimate influence on your destiny. Why not write to us at the address on the next page and ask for some free materials that will help you understand what being a Christian is all about. We would love to hear from you!

God bless you as you continue to read the Bible and let it influence your life and destiny. There can be no more positive influence on you or your family than God's Holy Word.

Back to the Bible is a nonprofit ministry dedicated to Bible teaching, evangelism and edification of Christians worldwide.

If we may assist you in knowing more about Christ and the Christian life, please write to us without obligation.

Back to the Bible
P.O. Box 82808
Lincoln, NE 68501